BITTER
MELON

4/27/15

First Published in the United States in 2013

MAHAICONY BOOKS
Brooklyn, NY
USA

ISBN 978-0988432413
Library of Congress Control Number: 2013911414

Book design by Khania Curtis

BITTER
MELON

poems by

ELVIS ALVES

ACKNOWLEDGEMENTS

I remain grateful to the editors of the following publications in which some of the poems in this collection appeared: A Morning in Harlem in *Stepaway Magazine*; Subway in *The Applicant*; River People, Stardust and At the Park in *Rufous Salon*; Quetzalcoatl in *Garbanzo Literary Journal;* Left Behind in *Colere*; Obeah Grandmother in *Caribbean Writer Journal* and *First Reads*; Blessings, and Morceau in *Lalitamba*.

This book would be impossible to bring to form without love and support from my family and friends, Otis Alves, Wynita Alves, Khania Curtis, Clara Freeman, Fidelis Ojevwe, Eric V. White, Dionne Dixon, Sophia Ward, Toren Curtis, Beverley Curtis, Rhovan Curtis, Joseph Kramp, Pangernunba, Laurence Berkowitz, Nicholas Prior, Judy and Howard Segall, and Eugene "Bernie" Kendrick. I am thankful for spiritual and moral support received from members of Lafayette Avenue Presbyterian Church, especially Rev Carmen Mason-Browne, Annette Leach, Selma Jackson, Peaches Diamond, and Edward Moran. I am encouraged by fellow writers, Keisha-Gaye Anderson, Tishon Woolcock, Cheryl Boyce-Taylor, Elizabeth Nunez, Anton Nimblett, and Caits Meissner. I am grateful for Peter Poulos, Jennifer Heron, Maria Felix and fellow chaplains at New York Methodist Hospital who do ministry with utmost compassion and resilience in the face of all that life offers. Last but not least, thanks to my former professors and mentors at Colgate University and Princeton Theological Seminary, Harvey Sindima, Nancy Devries, Tom Howard, Margaret Darby and Peter Paris.

There are so many more people upon whose shoulders I continue to stand.

Thank you.

for Marcel and Shelly Alves

CONTENTS

ANNUAL ENCOUNTER

I am waiting for you at the café for a late afternoon
rendezvous

Soon you will walk through the glass door and
casual entreaties would be exchanged between us
as usual

"How are you?"
Hug
Kiss
Some form of embrace

We will sit and talk about events that occurred in the space of time
since we last saw each other and now

Tomorrow, I will forget more than half of what was said by you,
by me

I will also forget the feel of your
Hug
Kiss
Some form of embrace

By then, though, we will have already agreed to meet again
at the same place, around the same time next year

I
BITTER MELON

EDEN

Come and stand with me
under the tree of good and evil

Here, we will pontificate,
elaborate on the meaning of these
days that fall and touch our feet

pushing carnal desires along
paths ahead of us

Paths leading to places we
fear to go until courage invades,
opening our hearts and minds

to possibilities beyond the gates
of Eden

MOON LOVE

Even the moon wanes at the end of the night,

Returning to where it came;

A rising star, with golden crown, taking its place: Champion of
The Day

Stay with me
Do not go
If you must go, do not travel far

I am a dwindling star of the night, unable to shine bright out
of your sight

I am a man of taste, of class, of dreams, some of which die fast
and others die slow

Even the moon wanes at the end of the night

Yes, indeed, it does

But some things are eternal like God, love, a comforting touch
or smile

Stay awhile and talk to me
I am a man of few words
I try to be a good listener

I work on this trait as a diligent farmer cares for his
crop in the field—because food and life are the same and you are
food to my life

I mold my thoughts around yours and respond only if I must

Let us grow together
Let our love not wane,
even if the moon must

BITTER MELON (ONE)

Therefore a man leaves his father and his mother and clings to his wife, and they become one flesh (Genesis 2:24)

I

My mother met my father at a dance party. Both were 24 years old. The dance party was held at a venue called Dancehall in the village where my father was born and lived. He worked as a police officer. My parents were introduced to each other by a mutual friend.

II

My mother was once engaged to the brother of the mutual friend. The mutual friend's brother, formally my mother's fiancé, died in an accident. My mother rarely talks about the accident. On that rare occasion, she says it was a motorcycle crash, failing to divulge details about the crash or the fiancé it carried through death's door.

III

On the night that they met, my mother said that my father tried to persuade her to come home with him. As if to encourage her to give in, he, according to my mother, said that he only lived with his mother, father, brother, and sister. My father's charms did not work the first night he met my mother.

IV

Few weeks after the initial meeting, my father was able to persuade my mother to visit his parents. People in the village took interest in the visitor. She was quite beautiful, a fact that was in contrast (according to my mother) to the other women that the police officer had dated.

V

The young woman arrived in the village, sitting on top of the handle bar of the police officer's new bicycle. She was a light skinned black woman. This aspect of the color of her skin gave the young woman immediate high status in a community that attached beauty to skin color, with the color white at the top of the beauty scale.

VI

The couple was married six months later. They were expecting their first child by the time of the wedding. I am the first child. I was at my parents' wedding.

VII

The verdict is yet to come on the status (good, bad, or indifferent) of my parents' marriage. They are still married.

VIII

Marriage is sentence to life with another person. Or, is it something else, more or less?

IX

I know what my mother tells me. I know more than what she says. I am the keeper of her secrets; secrets that words cannot breach. There is an unbreakable bond between mother and son.

X

The stories she tells have two actors (she and my father) and a reluctant purveyor, me.

XI

I am caught in the tentacles of my parents' marriage, recognizing that my loyalties lie other places. And so I share what I think is safe to share.

XII

My mother tells of the giving back of the ring, the need to have her space, and of the the love she has for my father, in a single breath. And I? I am the ever constant listener, hidden somewhere beyond the parameters of her thoughts.

BITTER MELON (TWO)

Woman, here is your son (John 19:26)

Diced pieces of a canoe shaped vegetable cook to perfection, green
becomes brown when tomato sauce mixes with minced garlic,
chopped onion, salt, black pepper, assorted spices,

dressed with oil bubbling in a pot.

Bitter melon is an acquired taste; something to grow into like an
oversized pair of shoes.

"You will learn to love her," my mother says, as she throws pinches of
curry powder into the simmering pot with the left hand and stirs its
contents with a wooden spoon held in the right hand.

The rapid genuflections of her hand remind me of the action of a
Hindu woman dipping and throwing specks of gold dust held in a
bowl atop the bared heads of jhandi flags as these symbols of faith and

good fortune dance in the wind, dodging the flakes thrown at them.

Bitter melon is gold of the food world that nobody desires, I think but do not
say aloud, wondering if my mother had learned to love my father by
the time I was born.

BITTER MELON (THREE)

...and the greatest of these is love (1Corinthians 13:13)

I was going to write you a letter but hope that a poem will
suffice, not in arguing my points—we, I mean, I, did enough of
that last night

You called me self-righteous
You were angry

We were out and I dropped you off at your place without telling
you why, that is, until you asked and I still had problems saying why;

The engine of the car making noise, speaking for me

The act of driving to the front of your house, unbeknownst to
you, to me, was visceral. The muscular memories in my hands and
stomach coordinating a successful sabotage of love

I apologized then and there. Ignoring the apology, you said that
you would remain the person you are, you won't change for me
and I should accept you or else...

You did not finish the or else (even though I wanted you to, I did
not push you)

Instead, I asked, what is wrong with change, especially if it is for
the better?

You called me self-righteous and that I have standards, high
standards

(I could have asked what's wrong with having high standards, but
that would have proven that I was self-righteous) And so I did not
say anything

You cried. And before we drove off to the bar, you started to
apologize for the tears. I said *No. Don't....* You asked why. I said,

because they allow you to name your feelings; Something I was unable to do

Maybe I need to cry more often, I thought to myself

The football game was on television at the bar. There were also a lot of beautiful women at the bar

You caught me checking out one of them. I said *I am paying attention to you; you are the most beautiful woman here.* I was telling the truth

You pointed out girls, telling me that the one with the afro is cute. I said, *No. She is not. I don't like her body type...too skinny*

You pointed to one of the waitresses (indicating that she is hot and I disagreed)

We agreed that the bartender was cute. I then caught myself, expressing the fear, *I hope you are not into girls. I told you about my last relationship and...*

I am not a lesbian, you hurriedly responded

At that moment, I remembered as we sat in the car in front your house you told me that you did not love your ex-boyfriend in a total way (the way that you should have)—flaws and all—and that this was not the case with me. You love me for all that I am

I appreciate your honesty but we have brought some baggage with us into what we are trying to build in terms of a relationship

I appreciate that you are able to lay out your baggage for us to look at I need to work on returning the favor

II
A MORNING IN HARLEM

DETERMINATION

I have passed the age of thirty without
marriage, kids, money, and society tells me that I should not be
happy

I am not happy
I am not conventionally happy

Modernity has gotten the best of me

I wear feathers of bright colors on my head

An anarchic city rules my soul

I am going nowhere
The familiar is too familiar and life, once full of joy, is that thing
that simply exists or once existed

I cry to freedom and she is nowhere to be found
I cry louder and noise of my own making reaches my door

I press on, determined to make noise and tell the
world that I am here

SISYPHUS

Oh motherless child
where will you run to?
Come eat the fruits of your labor
though they are bittersweet

Sometimes the world's broad shoulders
are unable to carry the turmoil
borne of corruption, leaving bits of humanity
hanging like dead leaves on an almost
bare tree

Falling prey to despair
Encouraged only by the instinct of survival,
we become the animals we were created to be

The stranger walks the night without friends at his side,
the hunger of an abandoned, orphaned child is his companion

Run to the river and lay in its wet bed
Let the river wash shame and guilt that have
accrued through the years: You have always been
innocent

Motherless child; death does not call your name

Motherless child; earth is more than capable of sustaining you

When the weight of the world is on your shoulders, do not submit
like Sisyphus

Push it off and run!

A MORNING IN HARLEM

Harlem morning, borne of
black flesh
Rays of the red sun bathe
roofs of uneven houses with
grace splendidly sweet in nature

Old men, one with a dog in tow,
hug palatial corners and talk
politics because they are politics

No rain or water can wash
the history of your hallowed grounds on
which names are written with the stain
of progress in process

Young and old walk boulevards and
avenues, a world colored by the beautiful
sons and daughters of Isis

Ethiopia's out-stretched hands have found
a home in your bosom as a spark
awaits to catch fire against injustice

The voices of your prophets ring true, and
poverty's reign is threatened every
morning your destruction is
incomplete

ANIMAL FARM

Cats fall from the sky
Thunder cries softly,

juxtaposed to heavy, drunken
howling of a camp of canines,

the dark flesh of night covering their fiery
crazed eyes

Cows and horses restlessly walk
to empty troughs long abandoned by

pigs, land-bound scavengers whose vocal leaders
stood on shaky soap boxes recruiting

members to the rebellious fold
with the slogan, "the chickens have come
home to roost"

MALCOLM'S JAZZ

I

The beauty of America is that she gave birth to you,
on the night of a torrential rain storm, in a field home to
weeds whose muscular stalks battled each other to squeeze
life out of you before the first breath

From the paddy soaked rice fields of the Carolinas to the rolling
corn hills of Nebraska, commenced a journey whose destination
was your demise

Cotton sheets covered the heads of men leading the way
on stallions heavily breathing under the weight of evil, causing their
backs to bend

Wise men did not appear
The North Star refused to shine, brightly

II

Herod's army wears emblem of a crow in the new
Jerusalem

Love of hatred and violence is all they know

Cry blood, Cherokee woman

Cry blood, Chickasaw man

Cry blood, Seminole child,

As you walk the Trail of Tears trampled
by galloping horses

lll

Rosewood—black haven turned home
to death running wild—from your trees
hang more than leaves

Rosewood, no longer comforted by black souls,
is left in the charge of invaders who patrol with
ammunitions that do not signal manumission

Horses lay basking in the sun; slumped over with
exposed cavernous stomachs stitched tight with

potatoes, squash, and collard greens rummaged from
fields once planted by black hands now hanging from trees

IV

One bright morning, when this life is over, I'll
fly away
      to
St. Louis, Missouri
      and
Boston, Massachusetts
      then
New York, New York and join
the OAAU

PRUITT IGOE

name that place in
the land of jazz.
name it in saint
louis, missouri.
hands rest in pruitt
igoe. hands that
once belonged to
children now holding
onto what is left
of life like the last
cornerstone of a
building before it
is razed, no longer
capable of with-
standing mass decay.
outsiders came. the
mothers welcomed
them to the land of
refuge that was once
pruitt igoe in name.
the fathers were not
home. the government
always has its say. they
give you money to make
you their slave. now you
are mute, hungry, naked
and without shame. now
you are addicted to
chemicals put on your
plate. a plate that shines
and blinds the knowledge
once seeping from the
hidden regions of your
closed, dark, beautiful
eyes. now you do not
see clearly. you are a
blur on the map of a
world steadily crumbling,
falling to pieces, pulling

you to your consummate
demise. you cannot run
from danger. you are not
lucky like the overfed
rats and multitude of
roaches that call your
home their home. they
can move; scurry from
death. you are stuck.
there is no place to go.
the grave has become
your palace. you live in
pruitt igoe.

.

III
HIP HOP

FALL

Cold morning pays witness to passing train across
dew-beaded window disrobed by the sun

The day brings fate pregnant with knowledge as
leaves dance limbless, in synchrony with the rattled

music of the train, and gather at the root of the tree,
giving life beyond the Fall

MUSICIANS COMMUNE

Music swells the halls of buildings
doomed for toppling

The bigwigs of the city have never
toured the commune before
condemning its structures for destruction

Big Rob stole into the refrigerator of
his neighbor late one night and made
himself a ham and cheese sandwich

The theft, the year's only, went
unreported especially since Big Rob
promised to reimburse the cost of the
food after getting paid for the gig on
Bourbon St scheduled the next night

The musicians scurried like roaches at the
approach of light to gather their meager
belongings before the houses came tumbling
down

They grabbed instruments first; banjos, trumpets,
saxophones, and old borrowed drum sets, and
loaded them into old borrowed vans and cars

The next day, the guys from the Fire Station came
and checked all the rooms for stubborn occupants
before strategically placing bombs to cause the boom

that made the walls cried while falling flat to the
ground like haphazardly placed floor mats

Nobody who lived in the buildings witnessed
their death; the pain would have been too much

Few months later, new buildings stood where the
old ones did

They were occupied by people who thought it below
their means to play music loud

HIP HOP

Breakdancing

Body breakdances its way back to
time the ancestors ran with spears
to kill evil they were unable to kill
because the eyes of the gun were powerful,
and far reaching

Similar to the floating temples of
empire-building that transported
black gold

The captain and his roguish crew
beckon a dance; *entertainment for*
you, martyrdom for me

Rapping

He is a student of the genre
His knowledge of rap spans
KRS One and XClan

How could polar bears swing on
vines of the gorillas?

He is the product of white
suburbia

Above his bed swings the Confederate
flag

while the stereo blasts the words of
Wu Tang Clan:
Cash rules everything around me,
C.R.E.A.M, get the money, dolla, dolla
bills yall

Graffiti (SAMO)

for Jean-Michel Basquiat

Oh native son of Ayiti
with head of mountains
eyes of rivers

The city is an eternal canvas

Paint *SAMO* on the
concrete chaos that is
New York City

Paint *SAMO* and
seek more than
the same

DJing

Cut it to pieces
Cut it out
Cut it down
I'm gonna cut her up
Who cut you up?
They had me cutting up
Cut school
I'm gonna cut school,
so that I can cut her up
Cut the grass
Cut the budget
Cut through the park
I'm gonna cut through the
park, after I cut her up
Cut time
Cut here
Cut ass
I am gonna cut-her-ass- up
Cut tomatoes
Cut traffic

Cut music
I'm gonna cut music and cut-
her-ass-up
Cut! Cut! Cut!

SUBWAY

We are standing in this shit-hole of
a subway in New York City

New York City is a subway
A dirty subway that keeps filling to

the brim with people thinking they are going
places but are actually standing still, looking
at rats the size of my hand

Rats that have more sense and enjoy life
much more than the spectators who are
simply spectators and nothing else

This predicament explains why people in New
York City—especially those that compete for and
are granted employment—enjoy looking at

rats scurrying along old, dilapidated, garbage
infested train tracks

Looking at the busy, overfed rats reminds the
spectators of who they are and what they do
9am to 5pm every day:

Locked in cubicles,
answering phone calls,
running to carry out demands made by the
boss

SOUL CITY

Today I will destroy the
home built for a king

Today I will rule from the
top of a mountain

Today I will beg you leave
me alone so that I can meditate
on how best to revolutionize

the anarchic city that is
my soul

ON WAITING

Waiting, sitting next to people, strangers
of night and day

Killing time by living connected to wires stretched
across canvas of streets and walkways painted
by the lost hopes of children schooled anywhere
but school

This city gives birth by spitting out of its canals
life forms cousin to the blind and unwanted orphan

The virtual has replaced the concrete
rat race

The sick has no place to rest their weary
heads

Solace found another home and fled

My heart will never rest until those who bleed
the sorrow of falling stars see tomorrow with eyes
of joy

I wait for this day
The expectation is the same the
day before my birthday when anxiety
floods my body like water across a dam
no longer separating two rivers on a rainy day

I am waiting but cannot wait any longer
because it is impossible for nameless strangers
to subsist on an unsalted tongue

RIVER PEOPLE

When the river dances,
we drown

Her power pushes us to her
bottomless bottom

Her children wear eyes
of fish, causing them to
see beyond the past and into
the future, bypassing the present

They speak an unfamiliar language
in my dreams

The decipherable chorus reads:
"You are one of us"
"You belong with us"

I wake;
My mind a clean canvas

Memory too has wings and can
fly above the flood,

consummation of marriage between
the moon and river, giving birth to messengers
to the living

IV
QUETZALCOATL

QUETZALCOATL

You never came. Someone else arrived, bearing your
name.

The people ran to him with gifts, not enticement to stay
but nourishment to keep strong, safe on the immediate
return journey home.

And to show that "you have what is here. Look. Dig. Go!"

But the visitor and comrades did not listen. They stayed.
Others came and they too stayed.

The plan was never the same. The child's destiny was handed
to him by a sword-wielding hand; cutting through lives

cutting through generations. Rewriting history so that those
who come later would only remember the victors and the lies
hidden in their truths.

How else can progress flourish? Civilization is spread with
guns.

Everything is the same; equal in parts like the rays of the sun
punishing a parched ground stomped on by the
powerful legs of a white horse, leaving in its wake holes
large enough to bury the dead.

This conquered land and its vanishing people waited for
you but you never came.

In your place—your surrogate—Cortes.

LEFT BEHIND

There are still people living in the village where I was born.
Many have gone due to the grip of death, others by the calling
of distant shores.

I remember the faces of people. Faces that were familiar to me
as a boy. Like those of the women who got up early in the morning
to pray at the river whose direction pointed toward Africa, a land they
have not forgotten with the passing of generations.

The women cooked food the smell of which woke the sleeping dogs
at the time of siesta.

As by no accident, the men came from the fields with empty
stomachs, waiting to be fill by fufu, fish, okra and other delicacies not
tainted, like food in America, by machines.

In that village, I grew not to become a man. I too had to leave,
following the dreams of my parents.
Not knowing that the burden would fall on me to make these dreams
come true in a foreign land.

SANCOCHO

Maria called and said that she made sancocho and
that I could have some if I want

I told her I have never eaten sancocho

She explained that sancocho is a Spanish soup made
of vegetables and roots and that it is healthy

I knew that roots was another way of saying vegetables
that grow in the ground like cassava and potatoes

I said that I would try it

And so I did; Vegetables, roots, and meat living and dying
in unison like the great army of Egypt at the Red Sea

whose salt content could only be surpassed by that of
Maria's sancocho

MOSES

"Bloodshed and tears" yells the man with a heavy tongue
above curious heads and strained necks of a gathering crowd

His tattered clothes tell a story not read by those who came,
like children at the mouth of a circus, to partake in the spectacle

"Bloodshed and tears" he repeats, a refrain void of verses and voices
that carry its meaning

But he who sleeps and rises with the new day knows that beneath
still water lives a revolution closer to him than his dreams and which

begs, like when God commanded Moses to go tell his people
to meet Him in the Promised Land, to cause ruckus beyond what is
perceived

May the Red Sea bury all evil within and without!

Indeed, every day a Moses is born, holding the secret of life in the
palm of his hand as a rod

and speaks a language not foreign to the youth who know the warmth
of blood before it touches light and becomes red and cold—cold like the

tears that flood eyes awakening to the knowledge of
that which is bigger than the self is truly the known self

AMISTAD'S COOK

Beneath the feet of
your captor, you bleed
corruption

Crossing over to the other side,
away from the shores that hug
your home

to be treated and eventually
become an animal that begs
the ground

Your fate and his are one
at death's door, with an
unlucky blow

Freedom too has bypassed
you

Your silhouette casting a strange
character in the shadow of the
sun

Evidence that your soul too has
changed with the act of betrayal

Taunt no more
Laugh no more

The final sound you hear
is the fall of your master

LEFTOVERS

I will eat you when
I return

I will throw you away

I will make something
new of you

I will leave you as you
are

I will love, I will hate, you

I will keep you in the pot
and put you in the fridge

I will not put you in the fridge
You will stay in the pot on the
stove

I will dump you in the trash
can

I will empty you in the
sink

I will call my landlord Maria
and offer you to her
and offer her to you

I will not call Maria
I will not offer you to her
I will not offer her to you

I do not know what to
do with you

I will neglect you

41

I will hold you close
and call you my own

I will disown you

I will spit in you
I will turn on the stove

and let you burn so that
it would be impossible to
eat you

I will not turn on the
stove

You will not burn

I will save you from the
fire

I will save you from my mouth,
my stomach

I do not know what to do with
you

Why are you not answering me?

I will leave you alone…that is what
I will do

YORUBA WOMAN

This land was not made for you. Its seasons bring confusion and conundrum beyond your control.

"The energy is too much." And so you sit outside the house in the hot summer night, welcoming the familiar and the stranger.

The former plays with your sister as she falls to the ground. The energy has overpowered her—I imagine—again.

Some of the women dressed in white run outside. They cannot take it as the scene inside boils to a tipping point.

Did the new Africa transplant from Cuba to these shores where you do not belong?

The spirits know the answer but do not speak to you, for you are outside, not even trying to look in.

BIRTHING

The gods collide when upon a face pregnant
with new life these slanted eyes alight. And
Cupid loses his way.

A greater force than this was never felt; causing
green mountains to grow green wings and
fly into the high heavens.

Oh, how the birds sing!

Their chants almost outdone by
ululations of trees, the movement of whose limbic bodies is
reminiscent of the fiery circle of the possessed as they
feverishly dance a divinely inspired dance.

Yes. The gods too ride the trees in abandoned, excited
ecstasy as the mighty hands of the ocean hit the cliffs,
causing green mountains to grow green wings and fly
away to a land as black and beautiful as your skin.

Yes. Out of the bowels of the churning ocean
come souls once thought dead, lost, gone but now
forever rising along with the tide.

So too is the nature of love because love is eternal like a
song unsung
a word unheard
yet utterly meaningful

like the first touch of a mother's hands on the
soft flesh of a baby she brings forth into a world
that does not welcome him but that he surely
must welcome because the mother created
him—as God created him—with love.

IXCHEL

The ocean speaks a language familiar to he who
listens to the intrusive crashes of her wayward waves
through the long night, anxiously waiting the new day to begin
so that Ixchel, with head of snakes, can appear and bless the root
from which will spring a child glorious in wisdom

Wisdom that knows nothing and yet, because of its very nature,
is all wise, all powerful

like the sun that bathes the good and the evil

or the crashing waves bringing to life secrets buried in
the ocean of life and placing them ashore at the place where was
begat the crowned king of Cozumel, an island not far from mainland
Mexico and where once lived Ixchel among the people, helping to
stave off the ruin that was to come with invaders disguised as friends

But good has remained among her now scattered sons and daughters,
Mestizos whose native blood fights for prominence with that born on
lands beyond the ocean

What remains live on in the tongues and looks of residents who stayed
behind, waiting for the chance to present itself so that they too can
leave at will like the tourists who come and go daily from the streets
and boulevards

It takes more than a drink from the well of the Earth to remain strong
when emptiness is all around

And the sacred altars—what remains of them—of Cozumel are
stepped on by those who did not witness the island's glory days
but are eager to pay to retrace the path of destruction wrought by
outsiders and time

In the meanwhile, Ixchel watches with dismay, storing up strength to
pass onto her children entering the world with a smile

PREPARATION

Same as it ever was
True to the rules of the
game

At last, like love overdue
or a dictator overruled,
in comes the past with giant
wings of waves

A priest turns wild eyes to the
heavens

Just then drops a creature
from the clouds with strong
cries of remorse

A crowd does not gather
Everyone is behind
shuttered doors

Only God knows what is
on the way

AGAVE PLANT

Agave plant turns to tequila, and all are happy
to be here on this island for another day

It burns my chest
My chest burns with the food the gods once
turned from because they knew that too much
of it was bad

Unlike justice, love, and other grand quests,
to drink oneself to death is not a noble death

When the Mestizo, short in stature, extends hand
with cup, asking me to drink to health, I drink not
to health but to the tempting nature of curiosity

I do not get drunk; I drink enough to feel satisfied by
I do not know what

At night I crawl under the linen covers of a cold bed
as the stench of cooked agave plant travels
through my warm body and I sleep to wake and explore
beyond its intoxicatingly sweet after-taste

V
PANTHEON OF ANGELS

AMERICAN APOCALYPSE

A heavy hand has befallen our country,
land of milk and honey

A light shines on a hill above the place surrounded
by hooded men

who came to do the job of the evil one as prophesied
by the Son of Man

We are the brothers and sisters of the persecuted
because we too are persecuted

Like the wind without name or the sun whose rays
refuse to shine, the same has been the same for too
long

We rise with the new day, meeting force with force
surviving by all means necessary

Our harms we will not let down but use to steadfastly
guard against destruction

We walk the stony road of life together; carrying each
other as the need be

Weariness is not part of our vocabulary

We walk toward the light hidden in us

We bring that light with us as we face evil
like soldiers at war

We fight
We fight
For justice and all that is right

in this American apocalypse

NAMELESS ABYSS

Oh that I may live to see the place I belong. Then I would be happy to
hold the hands of my fate.

Songs would burst from my chest as I welcome joy to a furnished home.

'Tis true, peace has a place prepared for those who wait patiently at her
closed door.

I am knocking, dear Mother of Creation. I am knocking at the bottom
of a nameless abyss.

With bruised fingers, I write my name not on its absent hearth
but on the bodies of my lineage. I pray for

more cries of joy than pain
more love than hate

My children will hold the noose tied upon their necks and pull
themselves up to the light.

SEEING

I've now become an unwilling seer who will grow old and appear to be a sha-man to the unbelievers.
            — Tanya Shirley, She Who Sleeps With Bones

I

"If I had stayed one more day in the womb
of my mother…" my mother says, as she
puts a juju spin on the adage 20/20 is hindsight.

Being born one day late would have let her
see far into the future, miles beyond the present.

However, instead of the 4th, she arrived in the world
on the 3rd, and so her eyes are blind.

She feels but does not see. Her dreams are void of
images. They come and go as fast as the day.

Her memories blow which-way as the wind takes them
away.

Nothing stays put. Nothing is nailed to her present. The future
is either mute or speaks a foreign language from afar.

"If I had stayed one more day…" my mother
says in the face of a surprise, sometimes smiling,
sometimes crying.

II

The one day has found its path into my life.

My mother's desire has become my own, without
my asking.

I see images from which I beg leave. I am the sole
watchman in my sleep.

I guard the gate of safe-keep, standing post

with nailed feet.

Yes, with me everything stays put, except for the
willingness to accept the gift that comes with

the day that passed my mother
but, alas, has caught up to me.

III

Your mother's weakness is your strength.
Many of life's treasures she passed to you
through the milk of her breasts. Recognize
and accept them as your own.

Once a miscarriage, her desired gift has now given
birth in you. Let it flourish. Put the gift in words and

spread it throughout the world. Like the trees of a forest
whose land was yesterday barren, let your talent sprout—
bringing forth truth, justice, and righteousness among all
humankind.

In time you will see the fruits of your labor. Use what you have
and not what you want. The latter may never come and what you
have is indeed enough to allow you to succeed.

OBEAH GRANDMOTHER

I

Buried egg rests
underground
Its final home
made of dirt

Its white shell
will eventually become
black as your face
and absent as the missing smile
from your eyes

II

Drums beat
in synchrony
with stomping feet
The ladies are dressed
in white
One opens the door,
letting the spirit in

"This is our tradition"
"This is our science"
You announced earlier in the day
to my mother, your daughter-in-law

She questions your dedication
to the Christian faith and you
do not expect this accusation from
your worst enemy (a rival, neighboring priestess)
much less from the wife of your youngest,
favorite son

III

My mother dances at
the opening of the door and
coming in of the spirit
Her Christian god unable to

conquer the African god

With excited eyes, you
run to her with nail
held in hand glistening with
the sap of herbal plants, placing it on her head

Transported back from
the journey, she rises
with a content, yet fear tinged,
smile on her face

You repeat, with more force than before,
"Our tradition"
"Our science"
The response is silent
acquiescence

BLESSINGS

I

Bless the child that does not
have his own

II

Bless the mother without a
home

III

Bless the people who sleep
under stars and
weep for food

IV

Bless the soldier who walks
toward the battlefield; May
he return wearing emblems of
peace

V

Bless the preacher, the priest,
and the nun; May they not become
the evil they lambaste

VI

Bless this land;
May she grow fruits of
justice and equality, abundantly

VII

Bless me—last but not least—
so that I can see strength in
weakness, the eternity of love,
and the power of the pen

CLIMB

Climb into the night, wearing suits of magnificent colors that shine bright above leaves falling through the weather-beaten hands of destiny gone astray while leading a lost dog on a street infested with decay

Secrets are underneath water beds glistening with the pungent sweat of animals that once ran wild. The guardians of these slippery fortes carry eyes whose strained gaze betrays the fear of the past catching up to the present as they yell "don't climb!"

But you must climb above the trees, the stars in the skies, and everything high, leaving low thoughts behind.

What has Athens to do with Jerusalem? Only he who seeks truth knows.

It is time to march toward a destination omen only speaks of; trees collapse, nature calls names of those who listen to her shrill cries of perverted serendipity, protagonists in the story of life are written over and over again by a hand not innocent as gypsies meander winding swells of roads disturbed by the harsh tones of music reaching beyond the confines of what it means to suffer.

Climb past the grips of fate—a fate that can give too much pain to the same person and is the purveyor of the inane.

Dismantle the token of luck. Hold fast to the truth that is never within. Carry a baggage light as a feather. Know that the companion on the road to discovery is no other than the self.

RECYCLE

We are marching toward the destination from which
we first came—alone, by ourselves, individually—unless
born a twin

Even then one comes into the world, from that world, before
the other who comes seconds, minutes, hours, days later
dead or alive

This life brings surprises that unfold and unfold to fold and
fold again like a song without end, recycling beyond and
beneath the reaches of the mind that swims in the mess of
its thoughts experimenting with meaning that is meaningless

We clap hands at the commencing of what appears to be a journey
on the road of life but that is in essence beyond and within the
reach of innocence :

A smile
A touch
A feeling

The will to survive beyond and within these happenings and know
that they are peripheral to what they signal and what is to be seen
in:

A smile
A touch
A feeling

And we clap at the appearance of grace alas like the birth of a child
pushing its way into the world feet first so that he can walk and spread
the word about the place he came from and eventually must return to

But for the time being, let us celebrate what it is that we are and
will become until the end when the beginning begins anew

KIKIYU PRINCESS

You are in the mirror while my
fingers circle your bare back.

Your skin is smooth, as I have imagined.

"You are pretty. Gorgeous."
Excitement floods your eyes.

Moments prior, we sat on your couch. You
showed me pictures of a Kikiyu princess.

I thought then that I was in the presence of
a Kikiyu princess in the heart of Brooklyn.

We played, we laughed.

I killed the gargantuan cockroach
that crawled out the rusty pipe of the sink
in the bathroom of your petite Brownstone
apartment at 4 o'clock in the morning.

PANTHEON OF ANGELS

Early morning brings voice of woman praying for fortune's
unveiling so that she could once again sleep at night,

mind at rest with the fast pace of the world that races around
and suffocates her like a hungry, wily snake or alligator at the
sight of an unsuspecting prey

She prays that from her quivering lips, to the ever listening ears
of God, words would travel uninterrupted

bringing more than luck to her bruised heart, long abandoned,
first by a wayward father who preferred to chase women other
than her mother, then by numerous male lovers

who disappeared behind the unhealed, scarred tissues of
her heart

She has found religion or religion has found her

Upon her head rest faith, trust, and all that is good, constantly
knocking at the securely locked chambers of her heart

How can she let God in when what she has given herself to
in the past has proven wrong in so many ways?

Thus, she prays in the early solace of the day for peace and
understanding that know no end

Her hope rests in eternity; if not in the here and now, she would
be healed in the by and by when the pantheon of angels welcome
her into that place, preceded by prayers.

BEAUTIFUL IMPERFECTIONS

Beauty lies in imperfections

At night, the stars watch
you sleep

Innocence and laughter inhabit
your dreams

Life has become who you are

You are life

Yours is a life in which butterflies
nest with ease

You pray for peace and all
around is still

The atmosphere explodes with colors
at your door

The gods wait on you, patiently

You are the essence of a presence
touched by that greater than the self
but that is the self

You are a conundrum unfolding to
fold again

You are here; you are gone and reappears
with a smile that does not fade but stays
to warm the depths of my soul like
far-reaching rays of the sun

You are the sun
You became who you are to change
into the person you already are

Stay you
Be you

Stay and be you, simultaneously

Kiss me and I shall melt

I disappear with your touch

I am in love with you

You caught my desires by surprise

I am unable to run

You grab me

I am close to you

I am here and see the
beauty of your imperfections reflected
in who I am, was, and will
be

STAND

When the world sleeps and
speaks a language familiar to
few

When the sky is no longer
blue

and the stars wane into the
dark

I will stand next to
you

BECOMING

I

May we unearth what is buried beneath the crevices
of the face,

and prevent dirt and shame to spread across a surface destined
to house light not seen through a veil pressed by hands wishing
to walk away from what they must first excavate

Secrets cause frowns not to vanish but fester like an incurable
sore

II

He wears prison gates on his face while freely walking
the streets

His dress is a costume purchased by the sweat of fore-
fathers who worked on fields owned by people that assumed
power belonged to them, until it was taken away violently

III

Sexuality marries into the outer layers of society; pushed
there by those who control morality

Let go and be

Let go and let be

IV

God created you and me
Look at Adam and Eve
They were let out of the Garden of Eden to
be comforted by those waiting beyond
its gates

RICH DREAMS

He dreams of making it rich one day

He wants a mansion with a parking lot
of fancy cars

He desires to travel the world, to see places he
only read about, seen on television, or heard
of by word of mouth

These foreign places include Paris, France, London, England,
and Tokyo, Japan

He wants to be rich and knows the rich does not want
to be him

He is a poor boy living with his mother and siblings on the
wrong side of town

He walks the streets and people think that he is cool

Selling dope is the only means of income he knows

His belly is not full

He is hungry

He is in love with a girl
who does not know his name

She lives with a man who beats her—night and
day

He walks the night looking for trouble

He gets into fights

One night, he bled so much from a stabbing that
he had to be rushed to the hospital

A police officer found him crouched over in the alley—
way, almost about to take his last breath

He woke up in the hospital the next day

His breath was spared

He recuperated to start again

This time, he promised himself, life will be
better

He continues to dream of being
rich

STARDUST

When the body dies, it travels backwards
to the stars,

providing nutrients for them to feed on, glow
bright with

as when falling to earth to shine light on the dust
we are

VI

THE INCAPABILITY
OF THE
SUSPENSION OF
MORAL JUDGMENT
WHEN THE TOPIC
IS RACE

NAMING

Go build castles where they do not belong. Take from the poor and give to the rich. Let the sun shine its face on all that is not bright— on all that is wrong with the world we call home.

Sing to the priest cloaked with greed. Give him and his church more than they deserve—your life.

You are the one to be taken into the woods and left among fallen leaves.

I will meet you below the tree. There we will stand, hold hands, and name animals.

WE WERE ALWAYS HERE

We are aware of the days we walked
long journeys without tiring

without pain because all that the
Earth gave we possessed and gave

back with ourselves, not worshiping
but living nature's plan pure and plain

Eyes straight, heads and chins erect,
courage emblazoned across broad chests,

we ran to the Queen awaiting the return
of her envoy sent with news of fate's impending
death

We pressed through woods to confront the
force which prematurely arrived

transporting bodies across oceans retraced
by disobedient, stubborn souls, searching

for maps to guide them to where they were first
pluck; fruits whose taste of destruction was unlike
any other taste

We used chained hands to climb down wooden crosses
hoarded aboard ships

and tortured bodies, beaten to stay put, to swiftly
jump into the mist whose origin disappeared not

into oblivion but into eternity born again and again like
the restless cry of freedom

TUSKEGEE EXPERIMENT

Cruel, honey-lipped, syphilitic—that is the South, Langston Hughes

Black flesh gone missing
in Tuskegee

Not worth the weight in
gold, young and old

Fetid smell in the air,
burning sensation
everywhere

Death loudly knocks on an
open door

Light dimly shines through the
window on the ravaged life
of the poor

There is no need to sacrifice
for the greater good

when life is abandoned decadence
that cannot be withstood

AT THE PARK

On this hot day, I sit to write a poem on
nature's ways and I am silent. Then I become
a listener as the birds sing and the trees sway
elegantly to the sweet melody carried by the
wind.

At the park, two friends strum guitars. Amateur
musicians they are. Dogs on leashes are walked.
They do not bark, gently carrying the walkers along.

Love is in the air, everywhere. Its product just
crossed my path; a child clings to a father's chest
so as not to become undone and fall down.

I come to this sacred ground to be one with nature
but we remain separate like strangers passing
in the dark without touching.

All of life is happiness. All of life is suffering.
Yes. Life is all happiness and suffering.

(Few Days Later)

Here I am, again. This time I bring an empty book.
What should I write? Move me. Nature, you are
my muse.

I come to you with dark spot on the
heart.

My mood is melancholy.

I sit on your lush, green floor and my soul
begins to come alive again.

I am trying not to fade into oblivion like the
years of school when nobody knew my
name.

At this park I walk without shame, unlike the original citizens of Eden. Everything surrounds me. I am not alone. I surround everything.

THE INCAPABILITY OF THE SUSPENSION OF MORAL JUDGMENT WHEN THE TOPIC IS RACE

Basmati, woman of my childhood,
you tell me of your black grandchildren
and declares in the same sentence
"but they are beautiful"

And I wonder what beauty means, and
how it looks, to you

Is it the color of your hair—once black,
now invaded by the white of old age?

Or is beauty the same as my teeth that you
beg of, because yours are missing,

long relocated to that place the days
are pushing you toward?

I am suspended somewhere between
obligatory respect and *"but they are
beautiful"*

Yet, unlike Kierkegaard, I do not
understand

LUCILLE'S TWENTY DOLLARS

Lucille gave me twenty dollars to take with me to Manchester, England in 2000. I was a junior in college and was dating her granddaughter

I ran to Lucille for comfort when her granddaughter broke up with me, soon after my return to the United States

Lucille had just come from one of her three times per week sessions of dialysis at the hospital and was lying weak, tired in bed but listened to me as I passionately argued why her granddaughter was in the wrong for letting me go

I love her
I care for her
We have gone through so much

When it was her turn to speak, Lucille informed me that her granddaughter was in the right. She made the case that I was her granddaughter's first boyfriend and that it is only natural for her to want to know "what else is out there"

She pointed to the fact that her granddaughter did not have a date to her high school prom

Needless to say, I did not want to hear all that Lucille had to say. But I listened to Lucille because she had listened to me

With the twenty dollars, I purchased a small wooden jewelry box engraved with the Shakespearean saying

"Love is that which passeth through the tempest"

Lucille was passing through the tempest, death leading the way

I complained about my tempest, making the case for a love I did not truly know the nature of

Lucille has since gone to that place where, it is hope, suffering does not exist

Memories of her stayed with me, including the lesson about moving on even when you cannot see beyond the loss

MORCEAU

store of grief

someone is unhappy;
unable to weep because
all her tears have already
been spent in the store
of grief

pennies for thoughts

thoughts are like pennies
falling from the sky on a
rainy day

well wishes on board

the boat has left the harbor,
sailing from me to you with
well wishes on board

i am you

people stare at me because
they see themselves in me

dust

i dig the ground,
searching for the origin
of a self i am fully aware
of

starry night

the stars never sleep nor
do they disappear at day, but
hide themselves in the womb
of the sun, waiting to born
at night

KARMA (NEW YORK CITY 2011)

I met a poet on Governor's Island at
a poetry festival. She was selling her book.
I purchased a copy and read it as the ferry
crossed the Hudson River. Someday, someone
will do the same with my book.

BITTER MELON (REDUX)

Imagine a tree

Imagine its leaves speaking

What do the arboreal
tongues say?

Imagine insanity above
sanity

Look within
&
beyond everything

Let the storm of your
eyes flow its course

Bring sin, bring pain
The fear of death is
no more

Imagine a world beyond
the imagination

Drink the cup of
wisdom

Drink it with the
blood of Christ and
see what happens

...headless Caesar

...unsecured empire

An army marching into
peace

———————————

Imagine peace

Wake up

Where are you?

Imagine life

Earth

Sleep
&
walk through the
closed door

The castle is beyond
your reach and Kafka is
dead

Blow your nose

Wiggle it and
make a wish

Pass the peace

Kiss the bride
&
give thanks for
life

Sleep
&
walk in your sleep

…me
…you

Hold it, taste it—

Bitter Melon

Elvis Alves was born in Guyana and raised in New York City, where he now teaches. His work has appeared in *Sojourners*, *Magazine de la Mancha*, *Heavy Bear*, *Small Axe Salon*, *Shine Journal*, and other publications.

Made in the USA
Middletown, DE
01 March 2015